Where Do Birds Live?

Betsey Chessen

Scholastic Inc.

New York • Toronto • London • Auckland • Sydney

Acknowledgments

Science Consultants: Patrick R. Thomas, Ph.D., Bronx Zoo/Wildlife Conservation Park; Glenn Phillips, The New York Botanical Garden

Literacy Specialist: Ada Cordova, District 2, New York City

Design: MKR Design, Inc.

Photo Research: Barbara Scott

Endnotes: Samantha Berger

Endnote Illustrations: Craig Spearing

Photographs: Cover: Darrell Gulin/DRK Photo; p. 1: Harry Haralambou/Peter Arnold; p. 2: Fred Bavendam/Peter Arnold; p. 3: Tom Bledsoe/DRK Photo; p. 4: C.C. Lockwood/DRK Photo; p. 5: Tom & Pat Leeson/DRK Photo; p. 6: Robert Lankinen/ The Wildlife Collection; p.7: Gary Schultz /The Wildlife Collection; p.8: Michael Husar /DRK Photo; p. 9: Darrell Gulin/DRK Photo; p. 10: Alan G. Nelson/ Animals, Animals; p. 11: Stephen Dalton/ Photo Researchers; p.12: R. Van Nostrand/Photo Researchers, Inc.

Library of Congress Cataloging-in-Publication Data
Chessen, Betsey 1970-
Where do birds live? / Betsey Chessen.
p. cm. -- (Science emergent readers)
Includes index.
Summary: Describes, in simple text and photographs, the different kinds of places in which birds make their homes.
ISBN 0-590-76967-7 (pbk.: alk. paper)
1. Birds--Habitat--Juvenile literature. [1. Birds--Habitat.]
I. Chessen, Betsey II. Title. III. Series.
QL676.2.C484   1998

598. 156'4--dc21   98-23988
                                                                                  CIP AC

32 31 30 29 28 27 26 25 24   08   10 11 12 13 14 15/0

Where do birds live?

Birds live by the sea.

Birds live in the desert.

Birds live in the city.

Birds live in the mountains.

Birds live on the beach.

Birds live on the rocks.

Birds live in the marsh.

Birds live on a pond.

Birds live in the woods.

Birds live in a barn.

Birds live everywhere!

Where Do Birds Live?

Birds live all around us! They are in trees, parks, gardens, on buildings, rocks, and ledges! No matter where you may be, chances are, a bird is living close by.

English or house sparrows (page 1) are well named because they nest in birdhouses and near people's houses too! Their nests are an untidy mess of grass and other materials, sometimes "borrowed" from the people they are neighbors with.

Herring gulls (page 2) live in coastal towns, harbors, and garbage dumps. Although they are almost always seen circling for food in the air or scavenging for food on shore, they nest on dunes, cliffs, and buildings.

Red-tailed hawks (page 3) make their home in nests high atop trees or even a saguaro cactus. Being open-country birds of prey, these hawks prefer large open areas like semi-deserts, with scattered trees and sprawling prairies.

Rock doves (page 4), more commonly known as pigeons, can be found in many cities throughout the world. They visit and look for food in streets, parks, and window sills. Their scanty nests, made of twigs and feathers, can be found on rock or building ledges.

Golden eagles (page 5) build their large nests of sticks, with a soft, fine lining, on cliffs or high trees. They live and hunt in mountains, grasslands, tundra, savannah, and rocky plains and cliffs.

Like a tiny windup toy, the sanderling (page 6) scurries up and down the beach chasing waves in search of leftover food the sea might turn up. It lives on the coast most of the year and nests in a hollow in the ground.

The horned puffin (page 7) is found only in the Northern Pacific. It flies high over water and also swims and dives in the sea. It makes its nest on rocky cliffs, boulders, and steep slopes.

The great blue heron (page 8) lives in both fresh- and saltwater habitats. It hunts in water, marshes, and on dry land. It nests in a shallow landing of sticks usually amid a group of trees or bushes.

It's difficult to think of mallard ducks (page 9) as wild ducks, because they are so common and not too bothered by the presence of people near them. They stay in inland waters like ponds and lakes and nest in hollows hidden in the grass or weeds.

The great horned owl (page 10), the largest and fiercest of the American owls, can be found in many different habitats, from rocky desert to coniferous forest. It usually uses the old nest of another large bird of prey in a tree or on a cliff.

The swallow (page 11), sometimes called a barn swallow, looks for small cozy corners to build its nest in. The bowl-shaped nests of mud, sticks, and hay can often be found nestled in caves, buildings, and commonly barns!

As we see by the birds nesting on a sign that reads "Bird," (page 12) birds live everywhere!